Written by
Sylva Nnaekpe

Copyright © 2020 Sylva Nnaekpe.

All rights reserved. No part of this book may be reproduced by any means, medium, graphic, electronic or mechanical, including photocoping, recording, taping or by any information storage retrival system without the written permission of the author except in the case of brief quotations embodied in critical articles and reviews.

Books may be ordered through bookstores or by contacting Silsnorra LLC at:
silsnorra@gmail.com

Due to the dynamic nature of the internet, any web address or links contained in this book may have changed since publication and may no longer be valid. The views expressed in this work are solely those of the author and do not necessarily reflect the views of the publisher, and the publisher hereby disclaims any responsibility for them.

ISBN: 978-1-951792-75-6(Soft Cover)
ISBN: 978-1-951792-76-3(Hard Cover)
ISBN 978-1-951792-77-0 (Electronic book)

Printing information available on the last page.

Silsnorra Publishing Review Date: 01/01/2020

Once upon a time in the kingdom of Kwaeke, there was a confident little girl named Ivry.

Ivry was courageous but very restless. Her restlessness kept everyone at alert. Ivry explored and experimented with everything within her reach.

She loved to climb trees and made a positive impact wherever she went.

Ivry likes to spend her time volunteering whenever the moment called for it.

Every morning, Ivry woke up early to fetch her mother roses from the village rose garden.

On a bright sunny day, after one of her explorations to the village square, she stopped by the rose garden to pluck more roses for her mum.

When Ivry arrived at the garden, something felt strange; so strange that it triggered her bird's eye view.

In seconds, Ivry's curious eyes scanned the entire rose garden. Suddenly, she noticed a heap of white mound that looked like an anthill. "Anthills are not white," she muttered.

As she got closer to the mound, she noticed a weird movement. The white mound rose, and before her little eyes stood the most beautiful creature, she had ever seen. It was a baby elephant.

"Please help me," the frightened elephant cried. "I came here to find help for my family and I."

"I promise I will get you and your family help, no matter how small, " Ivry said to the elephant.

"Now, come with me," she said. Ivry hid the elephant in a safe place and promised to come back early the next morning. She went home, heartbroken.

She stayed up all night researching how best to get help. Soon she came up with a plan.

Ivry went back early the next day to get the elephant as promised. While everyone including the palace guards were still asleep, she sneaked the elephant into the palace.

Screams of an elephant within the palace walls startled everyone including the King. This is what Ivry wanted. She wanted to get the King's attention.

Ivry and the elephant were arrested and brought before the King.

"Speak, My child.

What brings you before your King?"

"My King, I found this cute elephant in the rose garden. Her family was taken away by poachers who want to extract their tusks.

She fears her family may lose their life in the process, so she escaped to the village and hoped to get help to save her family.

With the help of the baby elephant, Ivry gave them all the information they needed for the rescue. The palace guards got ready and set out to rescue the elephants.

The guards arrived at the scene and found the elephants locked in cages, with the poachers were getting ready to extract their tusks.

The Kings' guards fought with the men and overpowered them.

The guards arrested the men and released the elephants. They brought the bad men before the King to face the consequences of their actions.

The elephants were overjoyed. They made loud noises with their tusks in appreciation of Ivry, the King, the guards, and everyone who helped in their rescue. The crowd cheered as they saw the elephants safe and reunited again.

The cute little elephant hugged Ivry for the last time and bid her goodbye. The herd of elephants returned home safely.

Ivry thanked the King and everyone who helped in the rescue. Ivry's parents were so proud of her when they heard the news about the rescue.

On their way home, Ivry and her friends stopped at the rose garden to pick more roses in celebration of the elephant's rescue.

THE END

Follow @ ivrydbook
to see more.